Birds Like Me

poems by

Joan Drescher Cooper

Finishing Line Press
Georgetown, Kentucky

Birds Like Me

ACKNOWLEDGMENTS

Publisher: Leah Maines
Editor: Christen Kincaid
Cover Art and Author Photo: Kelly O'Brien Russo,
        kellyrussophotography.com

Cover Design: Stephanie Fowler of Salt Water Media

Printed in the USA on acid-free paper.
Order online: www.finishinglinepress.com
            also available on amazon.com

Author inquiries and mail orders:
Finishing Line Press
P. O. Box 1626
Georgetown, Kentucky 40324
U. S. A.

Table of Contents

I. Fly East

II. Work West

III. Build the Nest

For my family and friends

I

Fly East

The Sky Holds Blue

Well after sunset. Dark clouds
veil one star, smeared
like mascara around an eye.

Crescent moon shines through
the haze. Dog Star howls in bleeding light,
through shredded fabric of cirrus.

Spring trees reach and splay
their joints, each appendage tipped—
sienna buds burn like embers.

Night sweeps color into its pockets,
like a fortuneteller waves over her ball.
Shapes lose edges. Stars sharpen—
black and white blurs to shadow.

Birds Like Me

Weighted like decoys
in the gray silt of dusk,
old ladies clutch

their purses—always
in the way, carts empty
of spirit while birds

like me swoop in, snatch
a can of beans, a lone
box of reduced noodles

roosting on the shelf.
So fleet are we
with our slim wallets,

buzzing phones—beating
our wings against time,
checking our watches,

while the older birds hunker
down, watch us flit the store
out of beady vulture eyes.

Catalogue

When my mind stills and I can attend to it,
I note the trees on our morning walk. Say each name—
under my breath, offer a quiver of poetry for each leaf:
sassafras of pond-edged leaves and poison bark, and oak,
too simple a word for the broad palms of white leaves,
shining faces of red, and the artifice of lacy pin dappling
the asphalt where our long shadows reach and stretch.

Maples chatter about sugared reds, elegant Japanese,
Ornamental Chinese, and stalwart silver—trunks that
bend with each storm. Pines of all commotion,
one sucked breath for each cone's grenade-like fall from
white, stalwart cedar, an odd Scotch, and odder spruce.
Sharp needle leaves tuck themselves into crevices,
slick underfoot. Sycamore, its spearmint leaves, a proud
cedar topped with silk fronds—the struggle of elm, childish
sweet gum spewing prickly balls to plague us.
A mimosa waves under the canopy of two-
hundred-foot pines and expels errant children.

A mountain laurel—ancient and twisted, lush and
sticky with white and pink cups when the hunched dogwood
dares erupt in light blossoms like skirted dancers bent atop
each leaf at the same moment the crabapple tosses its
abundant pink tears into the street. Long tapers of violet
bells, the creeping wisteria begs to be knighted a tree—
climbs twenty feet and strangles a valiant maple. Limbless
white pines guard a wild cherry and a small patch of invasive
bamboo—not a tree but shade enough, fills out the catalogue
that cushions our path and filters the sunlight under our feet.

Hunting Emily and Ernest

1
Light trickles through the trees
like a ribbon curling on our path.

The dog pricks her ears
and stops—points.

She stares into moss and pebble
poised—one paw bent.

Dives forward. Tunnels one-footed
and unearths a velvet pelt—

A mole struggles, blind and mute.
I shiver Emily's zero at the bone.

Tug at the lead. I end the hunt,
and we walk again,

Leave the corpse for foragers.
The light cold under our feet.

2
Each living room we pass could be
Hemingway's clean well-lighted place,

each garden, Dickinson's leafy haven.
As the dog pauses to paw at their moss,

Emily might watch from the window, a glass
in hand, toasting the coming night.

*Ernest, look. There's a certain slant of light
on that odd woman talking to her dog.*

He might join her, his brandy in hand, and ask,
Why do they stare at the moss in the drive?

He scoffs the glass. His wrinkled shirt hitches up.
Why not invite her in for a drink?" Emily winks

One eye, smooths a pale hand over her blue housecoat,
and nods. *She might make a good character*

For the book. What were we calling it?
Why not—Old Woman and Her Dog?

Condensation

The winter season you learned to drive,
we practiced at the park, shifting all six
gears plus reverse through thin snow and slush.
You dodged icy patches curving the trails and
followed the camping loops. Our laughter shattered
any serious error into minor, and fueled by bagels,
lattes, and my plain, black coffee. We kept it light.
We made up stories about the cold weather
campers and the ranger at the gate who tried small
talk after we were regulars each weekend. Suspiciously
empty each time we found it, a faded blue sedan
haunted beach parking. We tracked its movements,
tin foil covering the dewy back window and peeling
masking tape holding packed newspaper on each side.
We imagined the driver a smuggler, a murderer, or worse,
simply a poet. Why cold weather camp in that car?

We laughed after a few scares that winter—
a pony charging when the tires squealed on a turn,
a fast car on the wrong side of a deserted road, sika
deer nosing out of the brush, a lone osprey crying
atop a storm-wrecked tree, an older ranger who made
idle conversation from his truck but watched you
learn to parallel park. But that once, the murderer
poet lurched out of his blue sedan—we froze.
His massive bulk swathed in gray-black layers over
huge boots. Long brown hair, a curling frizzled beard
obscured his face. Mirrored sunglasses glinted in winter
sunlight—he stared back—at us. Stared straight at us
practicing three-point turns in the south beach lot.

And suddenly he was no poet, but a stranger wintering,
living in his car. He raised one huge mitten—
to hail us? We sobered, glanced at each other. He stepped
away from the sedan—we glimpsed through the open door,
an interior jammed—clothing, paper, cardboard, and plastic
thick and dark. After one gasp, you tossed your hair back,

and threw the car smoothly into second without thinking. I mopped up the coffee spilled on the sleeve of your jacket, caught my breath—and did not dare look back.

What You Cannot Understand

I dare you to stand back here in this place
you desire and grapple with the straining tiller—
yes, this one with jagged splinters and
aged, peeling paint—to steer the course.

This slim bark floats heavy in rough
water, but offers the only protection
I can muster. You ignore the compass—
and cannot understand the signs as they arrive.

Scoff at this rough conveyance, caulked
with tar and torn cotton, the bottom scraped clean
of barnacles but wearing scars from each
sucker. Each gaping seam leaks but swells true.

I dare you to steer this ragged course. Avoid
the wrecks while I bail and watch the fading
horizon. We list before the sails fill, catch the wind,
build speed, but sink a bit lower with each season.

Driving Home

Silent passenger
stares beyond her reflection.

The redbuds—tight fists
waving beside the highway.

Cherry blossoms lure,
tease the gaze from chaos

of thorny bracken.
The woods' floor dusted

brown with leaves, the old gold
of pine needles and cones.

Night Walk

The stars shine through
patches of clouds as if
someone cut a quilt square
out of an old dim blanket.

The fabric of the clouds is
rent and torn to shreds.
The deep blue night sky forms
a jagged arrow, directing me
north—east, out over the ocean
leaving the beach near Fenwick.

My heart follows.
The dog whimpers to go
inside, south to comfort,
routine and warmth.

Fight Please

Step up to the plate,
Just get to the field,
Sit in the stands, but
Show up.
Please?

When you shut down,
All the windows snap tight,
Each door I come to is
Nailed shut,
Painted shut,
Inaccessible.

All I am asking—
Put yourself
Out there.
I know I'm asking too much,
But that's my nature.
And you knew that
The day we met.

Foraging Storms

Lured by our first nor'easter after moving east, we
visit mountains of sand piled on the boardwalk,
streets flood, the traffic lights blink amber.

We find the winter inlet after a cloudy, early sunset, roaring
with pounding waves—they grasp black sand and rock.
Pitching madly in the dark despite a promised full moon.

Drawn to the power of a dramatic high tide, we climb
onto the huge rocks of the jetty, urged into the cold wind,
out beyond spray, then stumbling onto the beach to forage.

Deep swells mash themselves over the seawall;
crashing over barriers rarely touched by cold ocean.
The pounding regulates the heartbeat, pull and release.

In these untamed days, fishermen dare not cast, but
we cannot resist standing near the spray, the white splash
of each overreaching, shattered swell smashing the stone.

Clouds uncover the moon, and we spy bright birds
scuttling away as we venture to the black rocks.
Wary of the dog sniffing one step ahead, hundreds

Of tiny beings move as one like dark, sinuous ribbons
toward the frothy surf then fall back for the crashes.
The shadow of crescent beach protects their arcing

path through detritus left from last night's storm—
the deposited bones and shellfish, skate egg cases,
bulbous seaweed and tiny fragments of crab and clam—

pungent and fresh destruction, feast for the sanderlings.
Quiet, we observe their bodies rolling in streams,
racing toward the barely retreating breakers, retreating.

The birds skitter back delicately to watch us, one-eyed,

keeping sight of the dog who is wary of the waves.
Breakers crash, and they shrug us off to forage for fresh

fragments of the storm's gifts. Their legs are charcoal
angles; their eyes reflect a street lamp far up the beach.
Moonlight streams at us from the far sea horizon,

reflects in the bare spaces of shattered sea glass
the ocean becomes after a storm. Fine scavengers
we are, finding hope amid debris of such storms.

Moving East

Birds were flying away, and the winter was coming,
the noise of traffic and truth leaked into my midnights,
worried my sleep with sirens and phoned requests for rescue.
Someone told me, years before he altered his whole existence,
that change for no reason was a crutch for boredom,
simply destructive, but I persisted, hungering for it.

My mind conjured a house in the woods
or at some beach edge waiting for me to
loosen my spirit, and there it was.

The acorns are round,
Knobby and lush underfoot;
Winter will be cold.

A noisy place with high ceilings framed two walls of glass,
exposed beams, wide windows with shelves barely keeping us in, so
the woods can see the brightly colored glass from our collected travels.
From the outside, the house is transparent, curtain-free, exposed with
so many openings for the green of the woods.

Pines, mountain laurels, hollies, rough oaks, and sassafras,
barely outside, whisper their secrets of death and birth, sighing
together if there is wind or shivering with gusts. During rough storms,
the tallest pines are rubbery and sway against each other like dueling lovers.
The cedars that fringe the woods shake themselves and nod toward the house.
Grass is sparse in the shadow of spreading limbs, so damp moss
welcomes in patches a bare foot hobbling through the green world of
shredded squirrel leavings, pine cones, acorn husks, or barbs of holly leaves.

The acorns are round,
Knobby and lush underfoot;
Winter will be cold.

I thought I wanted rolling hills and sunset, but I needed a lullaby of woods;
this green confusion with the branches crowding each other,
the call of a crow or the skittering voices of sparrows and blue jays,

jabbering in conflict on the outside. The house is cradled and calm.
It is a good place to stretch and work the words, draw a line and color it.
It is a good place to welcome the onset of winter as the birds move south.

Winter is cold;
The acorns are round,
Knobby and lush underfoot.

Walking the Dog at Dusk

Yellow and orange leaves, first turning from summer green
        absorb the light best just after sunset.

Bare light from a sky darkening beyond the enclosure of trees is
        captured by the brightest leaves or
        swallowed by the great pines into
        deep green and black.

Staring up into the pines at dusk, every brushy arm of needles is
        sketched against a grey palate
        of fading light.

Headlights from the scattered traffic, now measurably slower,
        pass and flick on annoyed high beams.

They don't have dogs to rush home to and walk before the pitch
        dark, walks to wear a body out before bed.

In autumn, walking in the fading light with the dog is an excuse,
        the only way to absorb a bit of natural light.

The shut-in months are upon us and make us nothing
        more than silhouettes smudged on the glass
        of our hothouse existence.

Leaves Doubt

Outside the leaves shiver with huge drops of rain
that thrust themselves onto colorful ledges of near death.

Middle autumn rain is simply cold and rarely refreshes.
The fading leaves and curling impatiens hide in the
dusk of summer abundance—doomed.

Rain fills in the golds and oranges of leaves in the woods
outside the window from our silent dinner.

Stepping away from this autumn tableau, I see
the days growing shorter, and our tempers keeping
pace with the absence of light.

The optimism of spring, the hardy blooms of summer
laughter fades. Each leaf weighted with rain droops
and finally spills its cache.

Twilight enters fast. A glance at your brooding face
leaves doubt, as we enter the colder season and navigate
without words.

October Assateague

That Assateague Island morning
I skipped school last October,
monarchs chased each other across the road
into goldenrod thistles higher than my head.
Coming down the rise from the dune walk,
they crisscrossed before me. Mating?
Chasing? Playing?
Dancing with death?
How long do monarchs live
in this bright cold air?
Do they fly away?
Do they make the mad dash to airy
caves and winter in New Mexico like snowbirds?
Await their photospread for *Smithsonian*?

Dark birds float on flat water,
hardly recognized as ocean.
Deep blue, rarely breaks, and rolls
a gentle slap just before shore,
as the river used to do to the bulkheads
at home—shoving into them playfully
like children shoulder each other at the bus.
These dark birds—cormorants—not
the usual brown pelicans, hunt alone
comingle with strange seagulls.
The gulls look prehistoric, gigantic.
They glide over the water and spy
a spot to land and float. No diving, eating,
or scouting except for a place to
glide with the rollers just before
they nudge the shore.

I climb the steps of the new footbridge,
wild horse footprints stamp the dune
and trace the path of the elevated walk.
Pony bands retreat to the bay as the air
cools. A weedy bush blooms white—the

bayberry contrasts each bending stalk
of goldenrod dotted with butterflies.

Am I sad and mute because it is autumn?
This one, ripe day in October, is too good.
I want to ride the blue water and float like a bird.
I want to wander the island paths with the band.
I want to chase the flitting monarch and tease it
with my own orange and black body. I want to
struggle free of this form I have adopted.

Ghosts Driving West

Driving west every morning for thirty miles,
the dawn sky colors dramatically in the
rear view mirror and causes distraction—
all that loveliness missed for mundane work.

The routine of the drive is broken by ghosts.
Just after the county highways merge, a mirage,
a wraith with a long beard, and white flowing hair
from under a black beret, walking staff at his side,
waits an old man, soothsayer in the gulley.

The car veers as he registers, and I blink,
distracted by this figure, an eerie apparition.
Who waits for a ride on such a stretch? With
no shoulder safe enough, he stands in scrub.
Exactly what is he waiting for? Rogue thoughts—

out of the lush green, he could be mistaken
for foggy mist hanging about the fields. Other
nervous women like me alone on the road watch
for deer and patches of fog. After I pass him,
I check for ghosts in the rearview mirror.

On the two-lane stretch, sip at cooling coffee.
Further up the road, the roadside dairy busy—
move the cows during spring to get calves
moving and allow the grass to grow back.
A Guernsey, sweet but dull, attracts the eye.

One beast strays away from the rest. Solitary.
A student told me that the mind of a cow is one track:
eat, chew, eat, chew, and drink, sometimes sleep standing.
Cars fly by the herd, the morning traffic, a pastoral
reflected in the cows' flat eyes—the air, so blue and

bright becomes a charm of timing—renders me aware.
Perhaps because I notice the ghost man in the beret,

the new calves, my new rogue thoughts, and the bright
blue sky on a cold, spring morning in late April, the
hazard at Sixty Foot—tractor trailers leaping from left,

fail to rob my breath—I brake, and they cross unscathed.
I am insulated from mischance and poor driving, alerted
by instinctive urges to observe and meditate awake
not rush and chew, rush and drink, dulled to the beauty
of driving thirty miles west every morning in spring.

Over the Drawbridge

She eased herself into the damp corners of the old house
after moving closer to the water on a whim last autumn—
the smell of the bay invaded from sea breezes, the air cooled,
and rolling fog became her constant neighbor.

The fog kept its council with furtive scavenger runs—
it snuck into the yard and covered the scrub grasses,
rubbed cozy in the little valley of the rain gulley,
and touched the windows with shrouds of pillow fluff.

Erasing the alley path to the beach most mornings,
fog was an old throw rug tossed over the sand-spun streets.
Sometimes she drove through its curtain of veiled dampness,
surprised at the mist's absence just over the drawbridge.

She wore thick sweaters all that season to ward off the hugging
dampness that replaced a man's warm arms. A habit like a veil
worn for church, the house bedecked with fog soothed her—
eased her into the quiet of fog's muffled voice, a prayer under breath.

If the sun shone, she missed the tender goodness of his heat meeting hers,
but she squinted into the fog and forgot his warmth all that fall.
She eased herself into the damp corners and cradled the thought that
by winter, the constant fog for company, she might like living alone.

II

Work West

Domicile

Anchor the mind around a concept—for instance, *home*.
Imagine your domicile as it is, was, or you would have it.
Then ask the children to describe home so that the reader
Can see what they do. We expect warm, clean, and
Safe. We expect pastel bedrooms, kitchen cabinets stocked
with food, and comfortable couches perched on bright rugs.

One describes the noisy quiet of the empty apartment,
another, the explosions of anger when everyone returns, or the
threat from strangers who knock on the door after midnight.
Bed is the worn chair in the corner with the television on
twenty-four hours a day to cover the shrieking next door.
Bed is the couch in a friend's home just for that night.

Introduce the word *family* and brainstorm for a moment.
Married, divorced, committed, and disappeared. Every year—
*I don't know my Dad. I live with my steps and some friends.
I love my Moms*, but then the same boy calls you *momma*.
They confess fear of storms, bugs, dogs, momma's new boyfriend,
and smoke. They warn you not to drive down their street.

Home is a place to go to as little as possible and to leave early.
They join teams or mess up enough to stay after hours. Detention
offers respite and advice, perhaps a break on missing work.
They flock to afterschool tutoring and form their own families—we
anchor our hearts in this foolish dream of their far away homes
when they get back on the bus to be distributed into the darkness.

Undertow

The urge to write a lullaby for the shore is great.
So many picturesque vistas, waves crashing,
ponies ambling, children screaming and splashing,
but the undertow is also there. Subsurface and
fueled by the impetuous, dueling currents—hidden.

Sitting right in the middle of every sixth period
one year, a good year with sweet kids, was a sweeter girl.
No trouble, perhaps a bit slow to turn in assignments,
but genuine and earnest. Always a smile, giggles with
her friends. No worries. The rough boy in the back who
boasted of guns, and the failing pothead were my concern.

The undertow took her one evening. No red flag.
What lured her? Peer pressure? A desire to be daring?
Swimming into a dark chasm, one more statistic for
the opioid crisis. A sad, quiet death whispered over
the way the undertow sucks a casual swimmer
out and out until exhaustion takes her under.

Salvation

How many people does it take, to save John?
One guidance counselor, back from missionary work
in Appalachia;
two kind teachers, core subjects, of course;
one friend to plead to the first teacher,
another friend to take John home,
and that friend's mother,
 just naïve enough to open the door,
and let John in.

The first teacher and the counselor meet a tearful John,
so he can sniffle and promise changes
and then disappear into County lockup.
Back to school days later to skip class and hook up with buddies
leading to another arrest for drug possession—
and intent to distribute.

The first naïve mother shoos him away,
so the other friend, a wannabe, born-again girlfriend,
sneaks John into her father's house, which—
promptly burns down in the middle of the night.

The guidance counselor and the second teacher,
the bleeding heart, English teacher,
(No, we're not bitter)
give John and the family clothes and food
and information on emergency housing,
while a lawyer prepares to plead for John's ninety
days with the County to be doled out in
weekend retreats back into the system.

How many times do we meet with John's mother?
And half a step-father? Or is that half a mother and an absent step-father?
Or once with just a frustrated grandfather? John's druggie friends
lean beside the door to guidance and smirk when we meet.

So, John does his act of contrition and prays his changes

then French kisses some little girl in the hallway
instead of going to the classes he needs for his diploma.

How many times have we saved John?
How many times will we test our resiliency against his?
The sleight of hand in our salvation trick is foiled,
because no one but John can save John.

The War Inside

Walking the dog late last night,
to avoid the scorching heat,
the air was thick.
Every surface slicked
with impending rain
that would not come
until thunder shook the house.
Cicadas alarmed above us,
symphonic. The distant whir of traffic
on the parkway reminded me of the day,
the wars of the young,
their endless revelations—
sad beginnings.

The phone hummed in my pocket, and
unresisting, I withdrew it
and looked. Inside the blue box
a simple plea—
The kitchen stresses me out.
Can we ask for another job?
Maybe unloading trucks?
I answer for comfort
that does not solve
the dilemma—
We'll work it out. No
worries—like I am
a magic genie, wise—
and not an old woman
walking her aged dog
in the clinging, thick humidity.

Everything drags to a halt—
the cicadas
end their chorus,
a car drives by too fast.
The dog sniffs in the brush,
 the boy messages—*thank you, Mrs. C.*

I walk on almost rushing
the lumbering dog who looks
withered about the eyes and gray.
I consider adding cicadas
to the scene I am crafting.
I remember that it is October
in the novel, and the cicadas
will be tunneled into hibernation
in that fictional land of autumn.
There are deafening, singing insects
in this scene, a cavernous scene
with wars of such grandiosity
the common person cannot grasp.
The terror, for the foot soldiers are
children, teachers, and the few others
who can see it and choose not to
ignore it. No wonder I rush home each
day to walk the dog in the twilight
and think.

Thief

for Zach

Evening sky steals attention and then captures
      any hope for forward movement
      by deepening into purple, shading in
      layers that reflect red with burnt orange,
      striated by clouds, thinned and tearing.

She reads on about first blood. Almost retching,
      one listener bolts away to stand outside,
      another fixates on slices of sky, and all
      adopt serious faces to mask their horror,
      while she drones on and spills more red.

When we listen to the poem about the lost dog,
      my eye wanders from the window and
      another brighter vista back to the dog poet,
      her light ringlets, her dark glasses, and
      her heart pounding out fragments of joy.

Lessons

Autumn mornings, the sky explodes in the rearview.
Orange, blushing pinks, and violet ribbons lure the eye,
spur a rare sonnet, inspire a melody pure and true,
allow the mind to wander back to that glowing eye.

Later, a commotion in the hallway as you are reading
aloud to barely-settled spirits, some think it best to ignore
the outer chaos as an ill wind, a devil howling and feeding
failed hope for blessed order. But go and lock the door.

The memory of the bright sunrise revives the spirit,
makes one patient as order quiets chattering into control.
But beautiful distraction is its own charmed trap, so fear it.
Live each moment aware, firm of purpose, and bold.

Flawed Performance Haiku

One hiccup during
the Hallelujah Chorus
bass breaks soprano.

Intermittent burst
of laughter uproarious
young, stupid and cruel.

No red moon yet, but
sky's dim and blank. The deep blue
holds hue in the dark.

Anger stutters, spits
breath heaving, arms flail, windmill
against the vacant air.

Macbeth Breaks Down

Fuming at the side of the road, his car spilling steam
from a spent radiator, the hero vents his wrath on the
harpies who stop to chat and offer a bit of advice.

So, you witches seek to play? You have laid your
scabby fingers upon each of your wrinkled brows to see
which way the wind will blow? Well, be on your way!
Spread your glad tidings to the next, open-hearted fool.
I have washed my red sin in every pool, every spring,
in each muddy gutter of cleansing rain to no avail.
The blood will out every time. The stain of my deeds
rend my dreams. What good is it to sin for king and
country if the clanging of the battle deafens birdsong,
defeats peace with its echoing charge? You seek to
damn me? I am nothing more than a gibbering idiot
trapped by the hellhound I sought to befriend. Be gone.

Giggling like the mad things they are, the cheerleaders
pile back into their car, beep the horn, and speed away,
as Macbeth kicks his car, curses, and tries to call his mom.

Exodus

You must live
with your anger.
Hug it to you.
Polish its contours.
Hone its sharp edge,
until you make it a tool
for your eventual
illumination.

Moses,
You wear your anger well,
you find Him
in the burning bush,
in holy ground where
you cannot tread.
You fall down
on your knees
and question the flame.
The density of the answer
confounds—
I Am, I Am, I Am . . .

Hug that knowledge
to your chest.
Hurry away from the death
you made out of youthful
righteousness.
At least you acted.
At least you grasped
your anger,
your rough tool,
and struck with
a bare fist.

Now you play the prophet and
use the knowledge
of the fire,

the one that does not consume,
but does—
I Am, I Am, I Am . . .

You must live with the burning
bush. Hold it to you.
Carry its message
as it bids you.
Hone your heart
as a tool
for their eventual
illumination.

Your Blue Eyes

What would your blue eyes see?
There is a dogwood in the throes
of bloom in my way on the path
to work—witness all stages of bareness,
waking, budding, breaking. Today
an eruption into salmon—pinkness
those beaded curious eyes at each
center. Your eyes would water,
drinking up those leafy blossoms.

What would your blue eyes see?
A room overtops with furtive sniggers,
inside jokes encased in youth.
Pounce into the ring of their attention,
Drink up their energy. My heart hurts
at their fine youth. New blossoms barely
bruised by winds that will buffet them later.
In the window's reflection, I am fading,
shrinking and shadowy—
losing the bloom.

What did your blue eyes see? The stark
pine tree at the center of the path
worried us from the start.
Would our young collide with snow-covered
bark? Or skim branches as they careened
on wax-slick sleds?
Three generations on the gentle slope
that blinding white day of deep snow
and the bright blue, clear sky.

Before the youngest could take her second
plunge down the pine path, you were felled—
cut like a tree at its base. Straight back,
you toppled stiffly with eyes
Open, staring at all that bright, blue sky,
and lay framed by blemished, trampled

snow, you came to rest.
What did your blue eyes see?

Later in the hospital with the priest, after
the impossible nightmare, the team of men
carrying you, delivering you over the
snowfield in a wire basket.
I stumbled with the children to the car,
numb but I held the black, wool scarf I balled
up under your head to tilt your chin and
struggle to bring you back.
Children came, three generations, to gaze into your
eyes still mercifully open.

Your eyes were bluer than the lightest sky blue,
icy yet warm,
no hint of the grey you lent me for keeps.
I watched as the nurse swept a hand over
your blue eyes.
Had you fled to other visions?
Were there snowfields or blossoms?
What did your blue eyes see?

The Heart

"The Soul of the World is nourished by people's happiness.
And also, by unhappiness, envy, and jealousy.
Paulo Coehlo, The Alchemist

The heart,
which failed my father,
ceased
like a lightning strike
out of a blue sky
while we played in the
snow.

The Soul of the World
demands we listen to our
hearts—
these fragile organs
beating through the
lightning and the
rain.

After Father

What do you do when
the Soul of the World
begs you to listen to
your heart?

Your heart which is hurt,
resentful and bitter but
grateful
you still hear it.

What do you do when
the Speaking Heart fills your
eyes with blinding tears?
Forces you
to stand silent,
feeling the warmth
of blood in your cheeks.

The Soul of the World
demands you listen
to the mortal thing
that cannot think
but feel.
To feel your sin,
to feed your dreams
to taste the bitterness
of what is
Good and Right
despite the desire
for laziness and comfort.

Path

The path to the wild is a worn one—
Patterned with impatient stones,
Rough words and whips of
Overgrown, tripping vines
That tangle with harsh truth.
The path is raced with quick
Breath and burning thoughts.

I took a trowel with me last time—
I chipped at the corners of the deepest
Set stones of hurt and gouged at them.
You will falter on that path,
Fall and trip on the vines I trained
To ensnare you and distract you
On the way to the wild.

III

Build the Nest

The Story

First is the old story of the girl who comes to work for him. And she is bright and special, and he is dark and brooding. He is always bruised. She bruises for him so that they can be the same and withdraw in the darkness of a blue mood until the sun returns. Healing occurs when they look the other way. At each other.

This is the older story.

There is an old story of loss, either his or hers or both of them. It seems neither will enter into the land of the living until they find each other. A new birth. It rejuvenates all their relationships. There is hope for everyone in the face of their unlikely connection.

This is another old story.

This is the story of the brave girl who is surviving on her own. She is hurt or maimed but continues. She reaches out to one child usually who is as hurt as she is. The girl's bravery has no bounds. She saves another and heals herself in the process.

This is an old story.

This is a story of struggle—usually economic—the loss of a business, a house, a job. The character is fighting poverty that is chasing her or him. The desperation of the moment is the inspiration for some act that unravels the rest of the story.

This is a newer story.

This is the story of the loner who hates—older and set in his or her ways, not particularly unique. There is always an ingénue who is attracted—to the loner's strength, mind, status, even wealth—but who discovers a lasting attachment based on love. And love conquers hate.

This is a very old story.

There is the warm story of the girl who returns home grateful for his family's help and finds him there. She helps him out of gratitude, is transformed by her act, and blossoms into some climatic moment where she will either stay there or leave for the rest of her life.

But this is the real story:

There is a story of a hard, young woman who is loved by an artist. The artist dies—the artists always die. She is wounded, but survives, and enters into a relationship with a man who is just as hard as she is. She cracks his hard shell and loses her own. Their love is mingling and mature.

That is the story I can't stop writing.

Rough Sacks

Don't let me toss you into a rough sack

She decided at thirteen: *I do not love you anymore, Mama.*
Mama pushed her out the door to catch the bus and meet the eye
of every busybody and rough tongue on their street,
the morning her father slept with the window rolled down,
slumped in his car parked crazily, half tilted on the sidewalk,
sleeping off cocktails and snoring for everyone to see.

And whirl you round my head to fling you far.

She thought at twenty-four that she might teach herself
motherhood by practicing on the girls, his rattail collection
of daughters from past wives and accidents, before they could
decide not to like her or mind their father anymore.
She started with simple chores, duties, and discipline that fell to
cooking, cleaning, mending their clothes, and tending scraped knees.
Each clung to her, yet the youngest once shouted, I never loved you.

That is my habit—storing sacks of many sizes

She found, years later, a photograph taken the day they brought
her home: their only beloved baby. Beaming at each other,
mother and father smiling, posed on the walk where he would
sleep off a drunken night in the car the day she sat, red-faced
and sullen, listening to the busload of whispers and harsh
laughter, hardening her heart against the mother who loved her.

All shapes and roughness

After loving his girls, she remembered the car windows rolled down,
and her father draped by her mother's coat to keep warm overnight,
and the car keys gone—stolen away by his midnight guardian.
He snored softly, safe in front of their house where she loved him,
a giant of a man whom Mama could not move to avoid more talk.
Mama stayed with him despite the bottle and the gossip.

To dispose of love.

She fashioned parachutes for his gathering of girls, protected them
from their father's adventures. She concocted meals to lure them back,
fluffed pillows and made beds with downy blankets to cushion their falls. She
fostered a garden of forsythia, lilac and roses, thorns and wiry branches, so
when they frolicked away, the brambles might catch them and
bring them back for the lavender-red warmth of her love.

Don't let me
Toss you into a rough sack
And whirl you round my head
To fling you far.

That is my habit—
Storing sacks of many sizes
All shapes and
Roughness,
To dispose of love.

Circus

Home was a twenty-four-hour circus performance, three rings
with a mirrored sideshow featuring the tall, sad man,
one midget clown of a dog, widowed Jane—the grotesque
giantess with a beautiful face—three Tasmanian Devils
disguised as schoolgirls, and one little mermaid—
her long golden hair, twinkling sequined eyes but no mother.

Jane was drawn to the carnival attraction of the four little girls
wrecking the furniture, upsetting interiors, trapped inside.
She became their ring-leader, sideshow act, trapeze artist—all
after she met two angry, the others bewildered yet masquerading—
four girls hiding under the hollow big top of his manicured mansion.

Those golden little children, dervishes who loved her,
delighted at her somersaults and slippery turns, watched as she
avoided their father's anger and nimbly swallowed
the swords of his sarcasm. The stinging barbs
of innuendo which questioned her place, her ample proportions,
her bows to their applause. Jane trained the dog to speak, the girls
to fly as she blinded the roaring tiger with daring pirouettes.

Jane once swooped down like a trapeze artist once to defy death
by snatching them as he lay sleeping on the couch in a stupor.
Exhausted by their constant pleas for attention, he dozed
With no safety net to cushion his evening fall into the bottle.
Delighting in the danger, they thought of their father as a
fearsome lion that Jane did a clown act to distract. Spinning her
magic cloak to dart across the ring while the dog pranced, cart-
wheeled over pitfalls, and barked, she hid them in her big skirts,
so they could escape the show, cross the perfect grass, escape.

Four golden girls fed on the greedy, nourishing adoration that fat
women give the objects of their desire as they play the sad sideshow
act. His girls, her adoring fans with cotton candy breath and dreams,
imagined Jane the fortuneteller casting back their fateful hand of cards,
to snatch them from the tragedy unfolding in Daddy's circus.

In the Carnations

After the winter season and squabbles during the divorce,
an advertisement lured her with quick cash, little thought, and
acres of sunlight, silence, sweat, and flowers.
In the rows of deep red carnations, working steadily, she
gathered, stalk by stalk, armloads that paid by the hour.
Her mind wandered through all the little corners of her life,
called up by the deep crimson color in the tight buds.

The sky showed pale blue, tinged with red streaks that morning,
and the day grew oppressively warm—the air thickened.
The scent of the earth, which usually soothed her,
brought a vision of freshly mounded graves. Squinting,
she stood up straight, annoyed. She arched her back and
chased away fear. She thought, *regret is a shallow grave.*

In a stab of sudden clarity, she turned about to memorize
the beauty—both the full and decimated fields, the worn
faces of other day laborers, the tight bunches they gathered
splashed red and green, a bright sky piling with storm clouds
approaching from the east in a column of gray and black.
Her sensitivity heightened—peaked—she was full and ached
happy—perhaps struggling free from the weight of grief.

The feeling lasted an intolerably brief, ten minutes.

The sound of thunder rumbled over the fields as a shrill alarm
whistle blew before she could draw two breaths of electrified air.
They rode bouncing in the back of the open farm truck sandwiched
while clouds broke and rain poured over them, huddled like limp
bouquets of field flowers. Lifting her face to the pelting drops, she
watched the lightning cut the sky into jagged pieces. The storm flashed
beautiful—she wanted to weep. A woman behind her began to cry.

Rosie Visits Her Brother

Crunching over the thin layer of snow frozen into spittle
Embedded in the grass, her toes pinch inside boots too small,

With two pairs of socks that might keep her feet warm.
Rosie hears a wolf yip deeper in the woods, and hurries forward,

Slipping a bit on the railroad ties sunken into the descending path.
Being eight and small often bought her forgiveness for intrepid

Acts. A wolf would not understand that she was no ordinary girl—
She was older than them all—her brother Isaac, her mother or dad.

Thousands of years ago, she rode this same hill on the back
Of a glacier, carving out what the map named Appalachia. Rosie's

Laughter echoed in blue ridges and teased the wooly mammoths
During the years after the dinosaurs died. Sometimes at night when the

Trees creaked, and the owls hunted, she dreamed of the eons before this
Diminutive body became her habitat. She slips again on the ice-slicked

Rocks and scrambles for a handhold in the bracken. Chopping wood
At the bottom of the path, her brother stops as an unexpected shower

Erupts. He brushes the shards of icicles from his hair and jacket.
He grins and catches his little sister as she tumbles down the hill.

Mistake

You invite me to see the place you call a meadow, but the hollow just past the scrubby pines is simply a wild spot with overgrown grass and thorns. Thorns. They catch at my dress and the stockings I wore because you warned me to *dress up for once*. I could have refused, but I did not. I want attention just like everyone else.

You carry a backpack by its straps in one hand. Using the other hand, you push me forward—often gentle, but also condescending the way big men palm the back of a smaller man's neck when imparting secrets or orders. I am compelled over the bumpy terrain into the rough clearing. You say, "I love this part."

I hear the word *love* and a tiny lick of nervous flame ignites.
"What?" I ask to cover up my nervousness.

You frown. "Why do you do that? Why do you ask me to repeat myself when we both know you heard me?"

Then you place your hand on my neck and pull me toward you on a collision path. My arm comes up, and I automatically push against your chest. When I look up and see anger in your tight lips, I do push away.

"What I love is the expression on your faces when you figure it out."

"Figure what out?" I look over your shoulder to the places where the grass is flattened. Each place marred as if something large rolled on the ground and smashed the dry grasses.

"Your mistake."

Fluttery bits of cloth hang like colorful birds in the thorny underbrush. Fragments of other girls who dressed up to see your meadow.

Walking the Plank

The thin skeleton stands in the tall window—
paper blowing about the empty room
behind her, the window open to the winter
wind. A razor
poised at her wrist,
the plunging distance does not appear
far enough
for instant death—the straight edge in her
fingers her only recourse.

She washed all the blood from her hair and scraped
under her fingernails to erase the stench—
the grease of the garage floor on her hands every time
her fingers nursed the purple
welts around her mouth, the broken lip, swollen cheek—
throbbing temple.
The slightest scent of gasoline, dirty rags—
A man's sweat makes her gag.

She resists cutting at her own skin
again—an act that told her she was still alive
last night when she was drunk.
She steps onto the ledge. Only four floors up.
A trembling hesitation overtakes her, she
raises the sharp edge, shaking as if with palsy
and slices off a lock
of her long hair. It falls blond and silly
onto the floor. She draws another lock and
another lock just to feel the crunchy snap
of each strand releasing from her scalp.

It is not her hair; it was the golden hair of the girl
he traded off to two strangers
for cash, some booze, and a place
to crash.
The hair she bleached after her picture
made the evening news

and post office bulletins.

Her spirit sometimes feels dead, but she
knows it is still there
like the sputtering pilot light
that she studied lying flat—
her belly pressed on the cold
kitchen floor as a child.
 She knows and does not cut more
than her hair.

When she is done, he does not recognize
her—a battered and cut scarecrow patched
By bruises, tufts of gold blond
Left jagged that he clips off
and gathers up for trash—
her stained clothes and hair gone
with any evidence of them.

She locks into herself—tucked in a corner
and speaks nonsense as he packs
slim belongings. He shivers at the cadence
of her haunting recitation—the poetry
emerging from under her breath in time with
the rocking.
He shakes his head, grumbling at her.
I thought you were tougher than all that.

He gave her to a pair of rough men
who offered car parts, gas, booze—
some decent pot for his pretty girl.
Now he can hardly look at her.

He pulls her up and forces her to
dress by reaching for her. If he tries to touch her,
he can get her to do anything now—
a broken marionette, she is revolted

by his approach and shies away.
He spies the tremble in her hands, the broken
nails and the bloody lines from the experimental
cuts he watched her make last night when
he was high and called her *Alice* as if he
was the Mad Hatter at an absurd tea party
and not the true villain.

Intolerable Beauty

Right back there between the stage and the café tables
Right there while dinnertime customers loitered, fidgeted
Over coffee cups, waiting for her to play one more song,
The grandchild most likely to run away and crash into fate,
The grandchild most likely to burst into flame and burn,
The grandchild most likely to break all their hearts,
Kneaded the aged cramps in her hands with young fingers.

She leaned her face forward, and whispered over the hum
Of the crowd, *Grammie? Maybe I could play a little while?*
Shy blue eyes half-afraid to make contact with milky-green
Ones, she studied the intolerable beauty of their clasped hands.

In the back of the café, two women generations apart, hands
Clasped and whispering, bowed together. Grey hair waved
Down her back on one side, a profusion of blonde spirals
With strands of faded purple on the other; two sides of the
Same coin of time. Fingertips weaving over bumps and snarls
Of old muscle, sinews worked and limbered once by the same
Music. The intolerable beauty of one wasted and one nearly so
Captured the attention of loitering coffee drinkers and silenced
The knots of casual conversation as they stepped to the stage.

Rogue Tarps

When I was young, my father warned of rogue tarps—
sheets of torn canvas, shreds of sails with lines dangling,
boat covers that blow into the river to assume the current's
shape, a new life, submerged and lurking with the tide.

What I had imagined before brushing my five-year-old
legs as I waded along the bulkhead as seaweed, fishes,
or soft current became spectral fingers of dangerous
rogue tarps reaching for me, enticing me under.

That hot June just before you were born,
I swam every day from the Jenkin's Point—
racing past the two piers framing our property and
turning back at the edge of Fischer's place. My lungs

Heaved and slowed my pace. Like a guardian angel,
Mrs. Jenkins watched my progress as she fished from
her bulkhead and shook her head at the increasing girth
of you hidden and fermenting beneath my tight belly.

We waved to each other—nothing more than a splash
with a cupped hand as she saluted with her cigarette.
On the day of your birth, I made the turn at her place, and
gasped when something rough and heavy brushed my leg.

Mrs. Jenkins scolded my big belly back crawl, chiding,
Girl, you'll drown that baby yet! Then she cast her line, blew
out smoke. I waved but took myself into deeper water, half-
afraid she'd reel me in for daring to be taken by rogue tarps.

My Brother's House

We try not to talk about his vacant, black water house
as we glance through a book on a disappearing island
just a shallow swim away from his quiet, empty rooms
whose windows stare out into the creek through slated
blinds he installed but has rarely touched.

When you buy a place for the barn out back, he says,
take care to investigate the rest of the property, too.

My brother has a house he has owned for sixteen years
and spent the night in twice. Cutting through the party,
a loud guffaw over nonsense takes the attention
of the whole room. My brother rubs his chin whiskers.

He hesitates but confides, *an unsettled house is sometimes
restful*—no matter the ghosts, the mice, or rising waters.

Roost

Did I ever tell you about the night heron?
    That he roosts in my mother's smaller holly,
    the one that used to frame the clothesline
    with a birdfeeder for leftover bread?
    Truly the platform was more for the squirrels.

This annual visitor who stays long after he is welcome,
    roosts on the same high branch every spring and
    stares at us with a wary red eye, and never moves,
    never twitches that stocky compact hunch unless
    the dog, rustling for crumbs under the feeder,
    compels him to nestle deeper into the foliage.

But he is a transient, once lured by a neighbor who threw live
    fish to his brother blue heron perched on the green lawn
    like a watchful statue until prey or man presented game.
    The neighbor and the blue heron are long gone—bird
    waiting for the man to return years after his final stroke
    and the sale of the house. Still—the night heron, his black
    crown and gray breast glistening, haunts the green holly,
    serves sentinel in his roost, waiting for the next change.

When I look out the upstairs window and see the bird in the tree,
    all the ghosts ignored in this house crowd me like a mantle.
    The red eye of the bird watches, and his head bunches as
    spiky feathers with downy bases rise like the prickles of the
    hair on my head, the follicles on my arms. Something shivers,
    but I do not look behind. We stare without blinking, and I know
    my dead father sleeps in the easy chair downstairs, the absent
    neighbor fishes on the pier next door, my grandmother mumbles
    as she deals out a hand of straight poker then taps the card table,
    so her distracted sister antes up. Long gone, my silent grandfather
    chomps on a cigarillo as he trims the rose bushes in his undershirt.

Rainspouts in the Dark

I forgot the rain spouts, he says bounding
Through the house and up creaking stairs.
Not up on the roof now? She sounds pleased,
Cross. *At night?* She tilts forward in the chair,

Then she waves one hand in a queen's flourish,
Says, *Go on up there and help him.* Go now?
Mounting each step, my thoughts wild, I careen,
Foreseeing his fall to the hard ground below.

No matter his age or his spirit bold, my child—
Yes—he's thirty-one and a father three times—
Risks his life at her behest and leaves me cold.
Shivering in the open window, I spy his silhouette.

Looking up before he clears the leaves, he perches on
The perilous edge of the roof. *It would be a crime
To miss this spring star field. See it so clear and bright?*
He grins and my heart-wrench is forgiven tonight.

Little Brother

We played terrible tricks on my brother, the only boy.
He was youngest—a yawning five years between made
me seem superior. You dumped great clumps of sand
into the rear of his diapers, yet he played with his trucks
And never said a word. We were astounded that he smiled.

Bored with baby books, I showed him pterodactyls and
made up stories about them snatching up small boys.
Later he dangled his feet in the water hiding from dinner,
And a blue heron landed, stretched out boney limbs, and
took up vigil on a piling. My little brother burst through
the back door screaming, his tears were real—*There is a
Monster. A dinosaur at the river. A pero-rock-tile!*

We followed him down to the pier where his discarded shoes
Lay in frozen grass. My mother asked why, and he answered
That his feet were hot. The heron rose like the monster it was
Climbing back into twilight. I tried to close my eyes against it.

Fear of the bird—wings flapping, *a perch captured in its mouth.*
I stood petrified—afraid my parents would discover my cruelty,
by fixing such fright in my little brother—my ears roared shame.
But you, little sister exclaimed, *Hey, I didn't know you could talk!*

Considering the Weight of Words

Evening news pelts us, yet blind to the cost,
Countless unfortunates, we fail to see;
Clear facts suppressed, any commonsense lost—
Bubble and churn disaster's infancy.

One whispers the truth to a darkened room—
One snarls at news read by a robot mouth—
Heavy words quadruple free from the plume.
Analysts beg confessions from the couch.

What does a real person need?
A partner to listen without judgement.
Acceptance of all wishes? No small task.
Add sweet quiet—the listener intent.

Does all language deal a double dose?
Hide the truth to keep each simple lie close?

Hundred Year Wind

March wind ripped away branches, broke trees weakened
over seasons, roared all night and withdrew the river from
its bed like an unpaid debt. Stories of limbs fallen on unlucky
drivers, smashed garages, impaled houses, and that twisted
fate of a seventy-seven-year-old woman who met a falling
branch at her mid-morning mailbox warned us not to venture out.

Some spoke of hundred-year storms—five hundred-year events
during this rainless nor'easter. My sons marveled at the utter
draining of the river, recounting a fabled memory from a yarn
told as a myth by my father, gone fifteen years now, who boasted
of walking miles and mining the bare riverbed once in his youth.

The curious search for treasure, despite a buffeting gale force.
One elfin grandchild prizes up long-dormant pebbles, muddy
glass bottles, blackened sticks adorned with barnacles, and one
blue matchbox car my son remembers losing overboard long ago.
Her blue parka splotched with vile bottom scum, she cradles
Her finds. Her pale face glows, pixyish, blushed with mud.

By twilight the river sneaks back like a weak trickle of light
As the winds diminish as if exhausted in awed silence. The
sun gleams on muddy leaves, concave fish beds, knotty pilings,
sticks and limbs and curls of rope long vanished beneath the
surface. The wasteland of the river bottom shines duly, glinting
like armor, unpolished and rude, a warehouse of past battles.

Don't Name Your Chickens

My mother's people always had chickens—you just did.
Kept safe in coops, fed cracked corn, they laid eggs, pecked
holes in small hands and produced young when permitted.
Sure, one grew fond of them, but they were food—each one.

A terrible mythology tells of their killing—decapitation allowed
the bloody corpses to run until bled out and limp. Proud feathers
plucked, then the scorching. Lice running away from the bodies,
once up my mother's arms and into her hair as she screamed.

Remember, don't name your chickens. During breakfast, Mom
recounts again what it was to keep chickens, and how her grand-
mother wept all of one Thanksgiving dinner and did not eat—
her hen roasted on the family platter—that hen was Carlie.

When they were children, they named the creatures like we
do pets: Peep, Marty, and Bo. Remember Louie who
followed great-grand mom around like a dog? Yet each fowl
was consumed and every portion divvied in simple ritual.

First the butchering—entrails for the dogs and cats, necks
kept for soup or crabbing, the feet for jelly or pickling, skin fried
like cracklings—all the rest cut up and parceled into meals for five.
Each chicken, no matter her name, reigned the queen that quarter—

Fried Southern-style, drenched in buttermilk, dredged in flour,
egg and then four different spices (hush, that's secret)—a dash
of cayenne, ground pepper, salt, and plain old lemon zest, no juice
then drowned in a vat of spitting hot lard. Or roasted, skin browned.

Each portion large and doled out first to the men and the boys with
the old ladies next. Leftover meals sounded exotic to excuse the bits
remaining— a la King, Chow Mien, a rich stew, almond chicken salad,
but the best of all—soup. Hand-cut German noodles, thick-cut carrots,

A rendered base, rich with tomato juice squeezed and strained—
soup has its own devotional, its own clan. No one spoke during dinner.

Say no more. My people always kept chickens—you just did.
But my mother warns me not to name my chickens.

Saturday Morning

Spring onion sliced and sautéed with broken
wedges of last night's mushroom, mixed
with three eggs whipped to airy lightness
then dabbed with sharp cheddar, just
the remains from an afternoon party. One
bite without toast, warm from the pan—I
close my eyes—and I am eating quiche
for the first time at a sidewalk café in the city—
outside—not perched at the everyday table,
as the dog watches the fork leave the plate.

And the daughter, who is perched at the brink,
sober adulthood looming in her long shadow,
stomps around the house like an irate waitress
in the same city café, and prepares to leave for
work. She leaves most of the eggs that she has
not fed by hand to the greedy dog,
congealed on the plate.

Carmelia

Perhaps four feet tall, no more,
she ruled—with steely nerve—
our aviary of birds. Sharp-beaked
and button-eyed, Carmelia honed
our motley collection of wild things
into the pretense of innocence and
obedience the Franciscan way.

Never fooled, she pinned us
at our desks, pressed conjugations,
Roman history, instruments and
tables into our hands—dared us
to reach beyond safer cages. Under
the guise of class—two years in Latin
and one year of Trig served up six
semesters of philosophy according
to Sister Carmelia—*You birds,*
she warned—*I see your deeds written
on your faces. In the changing hue of
your skin.* Under her pecking gaze,
I quailed and pretended study of
tables—*volo, volas, volat, volamus*—
fiddled with the compass, but failed
to stare back, afraid she'd find me out.

Years later the humor of castigation
on a daily basis by a diminutive nun
named for the blessed visit portrayed on
every bare parish surface might amuse
me. But then it never occurred to me,
itching in the grey wool jumper with navy
blue knee socks covering my hairy legs.
To this day the aversion to navy blue,
white Peter Pan collars, and especially,
wool plaid jumpers haunt birds like me.

Acknowledgements

Many thanks to organizations that foster creative writing and teaching such as The Maryland Writer's Association, The Eastern Shore Writer's Association, the Wicomico Library's Light of Literacy Program, and Salisbury University's Lighthouse Literary Guild which reintroduced me to poet Nancy Mitchell. Nancy—I am grateful for your guidance and awed by your gift. I am indebted to the members of The Rabbit Gnaw Writers' Critique Group sponsored by *The Delmarva Review.*

Cover art and author portrait was taken at Assateague National Park by Kelly O'Brien Russo. See her work at http://www.kellyrussophotography.com

Forever grateful for my mother and father, Mary Jo and Lee Drescher, who gave me the freedom to explore and instilled the confidence to try anything. My daughter, Becca Cooper, you fill me with awe. My sons, Ted and James—so very grateful for our adventures. Thank you for supporting me and commiserating with your father. Tim, thank you for the time, the love, and the space to write.

To my family—please don't take offense. Poetry is at once free and incarcerated— the sentiments are real, yet some of the voices are composites of imagination and experience. Many thanks to my sister Patricia for reading, talking, and listening. Thank you, Becca and Pat, for giving unvarnished advice—sometimes it is wise to take a giant step back.

Thank you to friends and readers, there would be no collection without you. Much love to Danielle Green—former student, poet, and collection editor. Katherine Case, you ground me—thank you for being my friend and partner in crime.

Many thanks to the students and staff of James M. Bennett High in Salisbury, MD. Kathryn Wilde and Nancy Turner, you dared me to dream. Sharon Birch, thank you for encouraging me and always saying yes to a movie. And in memoriam to Karen Ezersky-Shuck, your spirit humbles me.

To my dear OLMC gang, particularly Mary Ann Kanis, Jeannie Tuzo, Donna Natterman, Regina Karwacki, Rita Doerr, and Susan Baker—thank you for over forty years of friendship and support.

Many thanks to Stephanie Fowler and Patricia Gregorio of Salt Water Media of Berlin, Maryland who fostered and published my novels—the *Lilac Hill* series. Find them at www.saltwatermedia.com or through the podcast *So What's Your Story.*

Notes and References

As a novelist, some characters come with agendas as soon as the pen hits the page. Their voices return with snippets that evolve into poetry.

Rosie Visits Her Brother—Rosie is six-years-old in *Lilac Hill Folly*, published by Salt Water Media of Berlin, Maryland in 2016. Rosie's continuing evolution will make another novel one day, but this poem captures her spirit.

Circus—an exercise from the *Birdsong Trilogy*, Jane is the matriarch of a Baltimore clan of strong women and challenging men that begins in the 1950s and continues through the present.

Walking the Plank—Unpublished, *Genevieve's Reach* is a science fiction novel portraying artificial intelligence on a collision course with fragile woman—a former runaway. Daphne must walk the plank on her own terms as she works with a thinking and feeling machine.

Intolerable Beauty—A portion of Jane's story from the *Birdsong Trilogy*—an unpublished collection of Baltimore stories.

In the Carnations—a cautionary story of miscommunication set on a flower farm. Inspired by a true story.

Mistake—A cautionary tale of a woman following her desire for love into the unknown—poetic-flash fiction experiment.

Joan Drescher Cooper is a teacher and writer living on Maryland's Eastern Shore. A twenty-eight-year veteran of Maryland public schools, she enjoys the drama and energy of her students. Long-time advisor for Poetry Out Loud, she regularly attends the biennial Dodge Poetry Festival. She was awarded the 2018 Light of Literacy Award for teaching by the Wicomico County Library Association for conducting an afterschool writing program, bringing live Shakespeare plays to students, and publishing a school creative writing magazine. She teaches English Language Arts Grade 6-12 and coordinates the Career Research and Development I course with Work-based Learning I for Wicomico Evening High and Secondary Summer School.

She distills the joy that living on the Eastern Shore delivers in *Birds Like Me*, a collection of intuitive moments stolen from dog walks, teaching, and dreaming. Moving to the Eastern Shore from Baltimore in 2006 spurred poetry, short stories, and fifteen novels. Short pieces have been published in online magazines such as Pandemonium Press' *Doorknobs & BodyPaint*. From 2014-2016, Joan published a novel series set on a West Virginia mountain, *Finding Home on Lilac Hill*, a short story collection, *Return to Lilac Hill*, and the novel, *Lilac Hill Folly*.

Joan is co-founder and treasurer for the Berlin Chapter of the Maryland Writer's Association, as well as member of the Eastern Shore Writer's Association. She is one of the Rabbit Gnaw Writers—a collaborative writing critique group sponsored by the *Delmarva Review*. Joan and her husband Tim have three children and five grandchildren. Her dog Hopper walks her daily.

www.ingramcontent.com/pod-product-compliance
Lightning Source LLC
Chambersburg PA
CBHW021156090426
42740CB00008B/1111